Hands Are Not for Hitting

Martine Agassi, Ph.D.

Illustrated by Marieka Heinlen

free spirit
PUBLISHING®

Library of Congress Cataloging-in-Publication Data
Agassi, Martine, 1966–
    Hands are not for hitting / by Martine Agassi ; illustrated by Marieka Heinlen. — Rev. and updated.
        p. cm. — (Best behavior series)
    "For ages 4/7."
    ISBN 978-1-57542-308-1
    1. School violence—Prevention—Juvenile literature. 2. Anger—Juvenile literature. 3. Hand—Juvenile literature. 4. Early childhood education—Activity programs—Juvenile literature. I. Heinlen, Marieka, ill. II. Title.
    LB3013.3.A332 2009
    371.7'82—dc22
                                                                                2008031412

Cover and interior design by Marieka Heinlen
Edited by Marjorie Lisovskis

10 9 8 7 6 5 4 3 2 1
Printed in China
P17201208

Free Spirit Publishing Inc.
217 Fifth Avenue North, Suite 200
Minneapolis, MN 55401-1299
(612) 338-2068
help4kids@freespirit.com
www.freespirit.com

A portion of proceeds from the sales of this book will be donated to the
Andre Agassi Foundation, which lends a helping hand to children in need or at risk.

Acknowledgments

Thank you to Andre; you'll never know the extent to which your generosity has enriched the lives of our family.

Forever thanks to my parents, Mona and Jack. Amongst so much, you've always been my safety net. My gratitude overflows.

To my daughter, Carter, God's love is ever present in you. Thank you for making my heart smile.

Finally, to my husband, Phillip, thank you for always encouraging my every dream. Because of you, I've become a better person.

Dear Grown-Ups,

It's a great privilege to be involved in the life of a child, whether as a parent, stepparent, teacher, childcare provider, group leader, or friend. It's also an awesome responsibility. Part of our job as caring adults is to instill and nurture values that will guide the child now and in the future. One of the most important values is a commitment to peaceful actions and nonviolence.

We must help children know and understand that violence is never okay, and that they are capable of constructive, loving actions—of making good choices. These are the central themes of *Hands Are Not for Hitting.* These themes go hand-in-hand with messages of love, kindness, acceptance, responsibility, patience, encouragement, perseverance, honor, and loyalty. All children can learn to use their hands to care for themselves and others.

Hands Are Not for Hitting is meant to be read aloud—to one child, a group, or a class. It gives simple, straightforward reasons why hitting is harmful and unhealthy. It encourages children to think about and practice behaviors that build a sense of self-esteem, self-awareness, respect, caring, responsibility, and fun.

At the end of the book, you'll find background information, ideas for more activities to do together, and resources that support and expand the book's message.

I hope you'll share this book again and again to reinforce children's understanding and appreciation of their own abilities. Emphasize that all children have the power to use their hands—and the rest of their body—in positive ways.

A big hand to you!

Love,

Marti

Hands come in all shapes, sizes, and colors.

There are lots of things your hands are meant to do.

Hands are for saying hello.

3

Hands are for greeting and communicating.

There are many friendly ways you can use your hands to communicate. You can shake hands.

Try it now. Shake hands with the person next to you.

You can wave to a friend.

You can draw pictures or write words.

I can tell a story with my hands.

There's something that hands are NOT for.

Hands are not for hitting. Hitting isn't friendly.

Hitting hurts.

How does it feel when someone hits?

It hurts a person's body. It hurts a person's feelings, too.

I'm sorry.

9

Sometimes people want to be the boss of someone.

Have you felt these ways?
Maybe you wanted to hit someone.

But hands are not for hitting.

There are other ways to let
your feelings out.

Can you think of more ways
to let your feelings out?

After a while, you'll feel better.

When that happens, you and your hands can play again.

Hands are for all kinds of playing.

How do you use *your* hands to play?

Hands are for learning—for counting, tying, painting, and asking questions.

Hands are for making music—for snapping, clapping, or tapping out a beat.

Can you clap a beat? Give it a try!

Hands are for working together.

Hands are for playing, learning, doing, and building. Hands are not for hitting. Hitting is never okay.

So what can you do when you and your friend don't get along?

You can try to solve the problem together.

You can talk about it.

You can listen.

We can build it back up again.

You can try to understand how your friend feels.

Your friend can try to understand how you feel.

You can think of ways to make things right.

What if your friend yells, kicks, pushes, or hits?

You don't have to fight back. You can walk away.

You can find something else to do, or someone else to play with, or an older person who can help.

Mom

my sister

Grandpa

my teacher

You can tell your friend, "Hands are not for hitting."

Hands are for keeping safe.

Buckle up!

Think of all the ways your hands can keep you safe!

23

Hands are for helping.

There are many ways you can use your hands to be a helper.

How do you make yourself handy?

Hands are for taking care of *you*.

They're for putting on pajamas, washing your face,
combing your hair, brushing your teeth,
and turning out the light at bedtime.

What do *you* do to take care of you?

Hands are for being kind and showing love . . .

Go ahead—high five the person next to you!

29

Hands are for saying . . .

Good-bye!

So long!

Kwaheri

Adieu

Take care

Zai jian

31

A Word to Grown-Ups

Children and Violence

Violence is deeply imbedded in our culture. All of us, children and adults, see violence on television, in movies, and in video games. We hear it in music, observe it happening, and may experience it firsthand. Sadly, many children experience physical or sexual abuse at the hands of adults.

Experts tell us that adults who abuse often believe they're entitled to have power over others. Feeling powerless in some aspects of their lives, they learn to use violence as a way to gain control. These beliefs and feelings begin during childhood. Thus, in teaching children about why people hit, the issue of power is an important one. As adults, we can help children feel empowered to make positive choices about how they'll treat others.

Hands Are Not for Hitting is a tool you can use to help children start to understand that they do have the power to choose not to hurt people. The book offers a way to help children feel empathy toward others, to solve problems, to control negative impulses, and to cope in constructive ways with intense feelings like anger and jealousy.

You can support this message as you read and talk about the book. You can guide children in other ways, too: form warm, caring relationships with them; set limits that are clear and consistent; provide consequences that are helpful and constructive; and model and express your belief that there are alternatives to violence, that violence rarely solves problems and usually creates new ones, and that violence is not entertaining or fun. Simply put, that hitting people is *never* okay.

Discussion Starters and Activities

Hello Hands. Talk about all the ways people use their hands to say hello: with a wave, a salute, or a peace sign; in sign language; or by shaking hands or cupping both

hands around a person's hands. Try the different types of greetings. Come up with your own special greeting, such as latching pinkie fingers or grasping arms.

Friendly Hands. Talk about ways people can be friendly with their hands—playing pat-a-cake, playing circle games, holding hands to dance.

Communication Explanation. Explain the word *communicate:* to use words and actions (such as writing or drawing) to tell someone something. Explain that we also communicate feelings through our faces, bodies, and tones of voices.

Talking Hands. Talk about different ways we use hands to talk. Then do activities that let you communicate in a variety of ways: Use crayons, markers, watercolors, or finger paints to write your names. Use charades, picture drawings, or sign language to communicate actions such as eating, sleeping, or building. (For reference books on sign language, see "Learn More About It," page 35.) Use your hands, along with faces and bodies, to show different feelings.

NOTE: Be sensitive to cultural differences regarding hand signals. For example, to many Americans, a thumbs-up means things are going well; to some, the same signal may be seen as an obscene gesture.

Talking About Hitting. Discuss the ways hitting hurts: It hurts people's bodies and feelings. It hurts both the person being hit and the person who does the hitting. Talk about why people sometimes want to hit—because they may feel angry or upset about someone or something.

Feeling Faces. Together, think of as many words for feelings as you can. Have children draw or make a face to correspond to each feeling.

Feelings Chart. Make a chart children or family members can use to show how they're feeling. On self-stick notes, draw simple faces showing different feelings. Write children's or family members' names across the top. Tell children they can use their hands to stick a note showing how they feel under their name on the chart.

Handling Feelings. Tell children that it's okay to have strong feelings like anger, jealousy, or fear. There are acceptable ways to show these feelings and to help them go away—ways that are safe and that don't hurt people's feelings. Discuss the ideas shown in the book and also encourage children to suggest other ways to deal with intense feelings.

Hand Hunt. Put objects in a box or bag, then close your eyes and use your hands to identify them.

Fingerprint Fun. Make fingerprint pictures using a washable inkpad and paper. Notice how each fingerprint is different from the rest. Turn your fingerprints into faces, raindrops, falling leaves, or stars.

No Hands. Put your hands behind your back for five minutes. See what it's like not to be able to use your hands as you talk, play, or work.

Paired Hands. Put one hand in your pocket and keep it there. Then try to create a clay creature or a block structure using only one hand. Or work in pairs, each person using one hand so that together you have two hands. Try a similar activity to play an instrument or paint a picture. Talk about how two people working together can create something fun and unique. What if the two people decided to fight instead of work together? There would be two angry people and no building, music, or painting. Take time to discuss the many ways people use their hands to play, learn, and work together.

Solving Problems. Ask: "Have you and a friend had a problem to solve? What happened?" Discuss or role-play situations where children might need to solve a problem. Come up with different ideas for solving it.

Avoiding Fights. Encourage children to think of different things to do in order to get away from fighting or other violence. Help children identify different adults who can help them.

Staying Safe. Talk about and then pantomime different ways to be safe.

"No" Talk. An important part of children's safety is knowing what to do when another child or an older person tries to get them to do something that doesn't feel right. Tell children that they can say "no" in a big voice, run away to a safe place, and tell an adult they trust about what happened.

Talk about the kinds of things children say "no" to (fighting, being mean to others, dangerous play). Encourage children to find words as well as hand and body gestures for saying "no." Discuss different ways they can say "no": "Stop it." "I don't want to play like that." "I don't feel like doing that." "I feel angry about that." "NO."

Help children identify trusted adults they can talk to about things that feel wrong to them.

Feeling Safe at Home. Children also need to know that they have safe recourse from violence in their own home. Here are ideas for children and adults:

4 Things Children Can Do If There Is Fighting at Home

1. Plan a safe place where you can go when the fighting starts.

2. Go to your safe place and draw pictures, read, or play a game.

3. If you don't feel safe, call 911. Tell the operator your name and address and that there's a fight going on.

4. Talk about the fighting with a grown-up you trust. If you can't get help at home, talk to a grandparent, an aunt or uncle, a teacher, a caregiver, or a leader at a place of worship.

NOTE: If you suspect that a child is being abused, contact your local Social Service Department, Child Welfare Department, Police Department, or District Attorney's Office. If you teach in a public or private setting, consult first with your school principal or director to learn the established course of action.

4 Things Adults Can Do If There Is Fighting at Home

1. Call 911.

2. Call a local shelter hotline.

3. Talk with a family counselor, therapist, or clergy person. Your child's school counselor may also be able to refer you for help. Low-cost or free services are often available. Keep looking until you find a person or an organization to help you.

4. Stay with friends or family.

Helping Hands. Use your hands to pantomime the helping activities depicted in the book. Talk about other ways children help or can help at home and school. Also pantomime and discuss the many things people do each day to take care of themselves: sleeping, getting exercise, grooming, eating healthy foods, and so forth.

Kindly Hands. Talk about the many ways people can use their hands to show kindness and love. When talking about hugging, emphasize that hugging feels good when both people want the hug. Let children know that they can say "no" to a hug and that it is often appropriate to ask others if they want a hug.

Good-Bye Hands. Make up your own special signal for saying good-bye.

Learn More About It

Because of You by B.G. Hennessey (Cambridge, MA: Candlewick, 2005). Using everyday examples, this book demonstrates the importance of each person in the world, showing how young children help and are helped by people in their lives.

Hello! Good-bye! by Aliki (New York: Greenwillow Books, 1996). A classic and engaging book about the many ways people around the world say hello and good-bye.

A Safe Place to Live by Michelle A. Harrison (St. Paul, MN: Jist Publishing, 2002). A helpful book for counselors and teachers to use with children who have experienced domestic violence, with a reassuring tone and illustrations that help a child feel safe and loved. A Spanish-language edition is also available.

Simple Signs and *More Simple Signs* by Cindy Wheeler (New York: Puffin, 1997; New York: Viking Children's Books, 1998). Fun, interactive books that teach American Sign Language for words familiar to young children, using clear pictures and hints ("like peeling a banana," "like pedaling a bike") for how to make them.

Understand and Care and *Talk and Work It Out* by Cheri J. Meiners, M.Ed. (Minneapolis: Free Spirit Publishing, 2003, 2005). Empathy and conflict resolution skills are simplified so children can learn ways to show they care, listen respectfully, and calm down and discuss problems together.

Your Body Belongs to You by Cornelia Spelman, illustrated by Teri Weidner (Morton Grove, IL: Albert Whitman & Co., 2000). Explains in simple, reassuring language that a child's body is his or her own and that it's all right to decline unwanted touch, even touch that's meant to be friendly. A note for parents suggests ways to talk to children about good and bad touching.

About the Author and Illustrator

Martine Agassi, Ph.D., is an award-winning children's book author and creator of *Hands Are Not for Hitting,* which inspired Free Spirit Publishing's Best Behavior series. As a behavioral therapist, she has extensive experience with counseling children and families in schools, residential facilities, foster care, and private practice. She has led workshops and group counseling in communication skills, parenting, drug and child abuse prevention, divorce, and self-esteem. Martine, her husband, and their daughter live in Las Vegas, Nevada.

Marieka Heinlen launched her career as an award-winning children's book illustrator with the original edition of *Hands Are Not for Hitting* and has since illustrated many titles for young children, including other books in the Best Behavior series and the Toddler Tools board book series. As a freelance illustrator and designer, Marieka focuses her work on materials for children, teens, parents, and teachers. She lives in St. Paul, Minnesota, with her husband and son.

Best Behavior™ English-Spanish Editions

Paperback (Ages 4–7)

Board Book

Hands Are Not for Hitting
Las manos no son para pegar

by Martine Agassi, Ph.D., illustrated by Marieka Heinlen

Hands are for helping, learning, playing, and much more. Children learn that hitting is never okay, hands can do many good things, and everyone is capable of positive, loving actions.

Paperback (Ages 4–7)

Board Book

Words Are Not for Hurting
Las palabras no son para lastimar

by Elizabeth Verdick, illustrated by Marieka Heinlen

With gentle encouragement, these books guide children to think before speaking, to choose words that are helpful instead of hurtful, and to say "I'm sorry" when hurtful words come out before kids can stop them.